POETRY MATTERS

Edited by Claire Tupholme & Donna Samworth

The Northern Counties

First published in Great Britain in 2011 by:

 Young**Writers**

Young Writers
Remus House
Coltsfoot Drive
Peterborough
PE2 9BF
Telephone: 01733 890066
Website: www.youngwriters.co.uk

Foreword

Since our inception in 1991, Young Writers has endeavoured to promote poetry and creative writing within schools by running annual nationwide competitions. These competitions are designed to develop and nurture the burgeoning creativity of the next generation, and give them valuable confidence in their own abilities.

This regional anthology is one of the series produced by our latest secondary school competition, *Poetry Matters*. Using poetry as their tool, the young writers were given the opportunity to tell the world what matters to them. The authors of our favourite three poems were also given the chance to appear on the front cover of their region's collection.

Whilst skilfully conveying their opinions through poetry, the writers showcased in this collection have simultaneously managed to give poetry a breath of fresh air, brought it to life and made it relevant to them. Using a variety of themes and styles, our featured poets leave a lasting impression of their inner thoughts and feelings, making this anthology a rare insight into the next generation.

Contents

Ormskirk School, Ormskirk

Polam Hall School, Darlington

St Leonard's Catholic School, Durham

Sale High School, Sale

The Grange Learning Centre, Low Willington

Windlestone Hall School, Ferryhill

The Poems

Food

Food is yummy,
Fabulous and scrummy,

My tummy rumbles,
My tummy grumbles,

Without its fill,
It moans until,

Sausage and mash,
That lovely nosh,

Gravy on top,
Piping hot,

Followed by,
Warm apple pie,

With custard runny,
Yellow and sunny,

It's all a dream,
Not what it seems,

Mum's just gone to the shop,
I hope she's quick I'm fit to drop,

Tasty food is on the way,
Rushing down the motorway,

There she is, she's back,
There's food to fill that empty rack,

Food is piled onto my plate, hooray,
Oh I forgot, it's cabbage today!

Joe Gutteridge [12]
Appleby Grammar School, Appleby

What Matters To Me?

What matters to me is keeping fit,
Having fun, participating, watching it.
The whistle of the racket, the roar of the crowd,
'Goal', he says out loud.
Starting up, falling down the progression,
The sad expression feeling proud.

The kick of the bass, screams from the crowd,
The sound before the animal that is the song gets disembowelled.
Feel the drums come from within your chest,
Move to the chill out tent, have a rest.
Feel the pulse rattle your bones,
It doesn't matter, speakers or headphones.

My family are my harness for if I should fall.
They are the greatest and I love them all.
My friends provide company, support and trust.
Keep my friends that's a must
And hope our friendship doesn't rust.
Sport, music, friends and family
These are the things that matter to me.

Sam Taylor (11)
Appleby Grammar School, Appleby

What Matters To Me

So, what matters to me?
It's the glint in my eye at the hint of a chance,
Running like a puppy bound by a trance.
It's the sight of the beady eyes scanning the field,
I'm the hero, a knight in armour, sword and shield.
It's the clap, clap, clap of people cheering me,
For my great performance that left them shining with glee
The sun is a furnace, glowing in the sky,
I wipe my forehead with sweat, pouring from the shine.
Football.

So, what matters to me?
It's the flutter of a page and the crunch of a biscuit,
Only biscuits for dunking are fit for it.
It's a delicious warming sun melting in my mouth,
It's never loud in the kitchen, no cries or shouts.
The whistle of the kettle means there's another cuppa,
My book and biscuit drop, I always leave a clutter.
The sweet milky liquid runs down my throat,
I spill it on the page, then wipe it with my coat.
Reading.

So, what matters to me?
It's the warming embrace of someone that loves me,
They're always there to hug mo, to make me feel free.
They're a cool breeze on my face on a summer's day,
Every single day loving, 'I love you', they say.
Cheering in my football games, and when I'm in shame.
I hang my head, but they still clap me all the same.
They make me feel happy, even when I'm feeling sad,
They're a net for me to fall on when I'm going mad.
Family

Lawrence Howard (12)
Appleby Grammar School, Appleby

What Matters To Me

My best friend
The king of the night
Like a free spirit
And so cute in the light,
As black as soot
All the way
From head to foot
Half-tame, half-wild
And his best friend is me, a child
My best friend is a cat.

As sweet as a summer's day
As soft as a bed of hay
Safe and calming
And not alarming.
As fun as a puppy
All cute and fluffy
As swift as a dove
They have all my love
This is my family.

Fun and daring
Away from home
And not really caring.
A taste of something new
A place all different
With a hundred things to do.
Hot or cold, new or old
Languages odd
We reply with a nod
That's why holidays matter to me.

Georgia Cross (11)
Appleby Grammar School, Appleby

What Matters To Me

What matters to me are my family,
Like cushions, they're always there for me.
I love them and they love me,
It's the way we'll always be.
My mum is kind, she makes my tea.
My dad is smart, he teaches me.
My brother's weird, but good fun too.
My family is what matters to me!

What matters to me are my friends,
I can always talk to them.
If I ask them for help, they always say OK.
They care for me, but in a different way.
We are friends through thick and thin.
We laugh and cheer and chatter.
To me friends are what matter!

What matters to me are my pets,
Buying them I have no regrets.
They're great entertainment, they're fun.
In the pet show my dog won.
My hamster, Holly, is cute and petite,
I got her on Christmas Day.
I love my pets, they're the best,
What matters to me are my pets!

Laura Brice (11)
Appleby Grammar School, Appleby

What Matters To Me

My family and friends
Are what matter to me.
It's so good to have them,
It helps you be free.
When you feel down,
They cheer you right up,
As high as a tree.

A knight on his horse,
Sword gleaming in hand.
One of the finest,
In all of the land.
He goes into battle,
So proud to be.
Part of the team.
For this is rugby.

I love my bike,
Pedal and motor.
I love to zoom,
Around like a rotor.
Down the road,
Through a puddle. Splash!
Hopefully not hitting,
A lamppost *Crash!*

Edward Dale (12)
Appleby Grammar School, Appleby

Things That Matter To Me

The Internet is a good place to be,
You can use it on your Wii.
But watch out for strangers,
As sly as a fox,
With them around there could be dangers.

The roar of the crowd,
Is just so loud!
I am talking about cricket,
'Bowler, knock over that wicket!'
When that bat slaps the ball,
You know they have no chance at all!

The ruffle of pages,
Has been heard for ages.
Reading refreshes you after TV.
Or indeed the PS3.
It takes you into another world,
Through the pages you've just curled.
These are the things that matter to me,
And I find them as great as can be!

Peter Rodger (11)
Appleby Grammar Cohool, Appleby

What Matters To Me

Of all the things I like I guess,
These are the things I like the best.
When work is done and it's time to play,
This is how I spend my day.

With sturdy boots and a heavy sack,
I set off on an uphill track.
Amazing views unfold around,
I pause to take in the sights and sounds.
Singing birds, a glassy lake,
A perfect spot for a well-earned break.

Feeling the wind whip against my face,
Pushing against in a hard-fought race.
Panting breathless a rosy glow,
Keep the pace going, not far to go.
Flowing with pride as I cross the line,
Hold up the trophy, let it shine.

Time to relax and have some fun,
Nintendo is my number one.
Fingers pumping, buttons clicking,
Donkey Kong and Mario whistling,
Round the track, in a lightning flash,
Avoiding mushrooms in my path.

Cooker warming, apron on,
Time to make some Sunday scones.
Kneading, squashing, rolling out,
'Are they ready?' the family shout.
Out of the oven, onto a plate,
Melting mouthfuls, 'Wow, they're great'!

Curled up snug in my bed,
No thoughts of homework in my head.
Cosy, warm duvet wrapped,
A lovely day with an afternoon nap.
The smell of hot chocolate coming my way,
How I love a pyjama day.

Emma Dunham (12)
Appleby Grammar School, Appleby

What Matters To Me?

Life is very important, but not just about me,
The most important things are my friends and family,
Friends make me laugh and make me smile,
They care, they think, they make me happy,
Families are the same, but different in a way,
They care, they think, they make me happy
But they look after me in a different way,
They teach me love, life and happiness.

If you know me, I love my sport,
Badminton comes in at my number three, on that court,
Second is cricket, captain of Appleby,
Oh that's me,
But now it's the knight in shining armour,
For me it's Bolton and Carlisle,
Appleby also up there in that category,
Especially under 13's with me,
Zoom goes the ball into the net,
It's football, you'll bet.

What matters to me,
Is that I live life to the full,
Take risks, relax,
Do new stuff,
Explore places,
That's what you need,
Overall this is my life and
That's what matter's to me!

Abe Butterworth [11]
Appleby Grammar School, Appleby

What Matters To Me

What matters to me is music,
Especially pop,
When I go into Carlisle I stroll in HMV,
My favourite music shop,
I always buy a new album,
So I dance and sing,
Then my friends come over,
And have a sort of party thing.

My chestnut friend,
Like a firework exploding,
With no end,
I'm actually talking about my pony, Zoey,
The latest addition to my family.

Now let's move on to family and friends,
Friends I can trust,
Swap the latest trends,
My family are always there,
Making me happy when I think it's not fair.

This is the end of my poem,
So I hope you found out loads about me!

Marima Idle (12)
Appleby Grammar School, Appleby

What Matters To Me

What matters to me
It's dancing you see
Performing for you
Hope you like it too
When the beat runs through me
I feel so free

Being in the past
Wearing the clothes that they once wore
Before you were born
I'm always Mary, the kitchen maid
Preparing the food when the master says
Pretending to live the lives that they once lived

Tilly, my hot-water bottle
The best toy in the basket
A constant chatterbox
A pickpocket in disguise
But a little adventurer
That is my cat Tilly.

Hannah Roberts (11)
Appleby Grammar School, Appleby

We Are The Best

Yet another football game,
Wattsfield is the opposition's name.
We've all been training really hard,
We hope we don't get a coloured card.

It is a very important match,
So our keeper has practised to catch.
We walked out onto the field,
To beat Wattsfield and win the shield.

We have kicked off at 12 noon,
And hopefully we'll get a goal soon.
Our striker shoots and scores,
Our supporters go crazy and starts to roar.

Two more goals to our team,
One penalty to them which was very mean.
He was not fouled he just pretended,
Our team and crowd were all offended.

'Cheat, cheat, cheat!' they all cried,
The Wattsfield player tried to hide.
He put the ball onto the spot
He shoots and scores with a lucky shot.

3-1 is the half-time score,
No way is this game a great big bore.
To put this game to bed,
We must start to use our head.

It started well in the second half
Their striker got an injured calf.
They struggled on to keep the ball,
Our players were like a brick wall.

The game finally came to an end
Appleby's u13s were champions again.
Our captain Ross collected the shield,
And all the opposition left the field.

The supporters were oh so proud,
And they were singing out very loud.
'Appleby, Appleby you are the best,
You are better than all the rest'.

Ross Parkin (12)
Appleby Grammar School, Appleby

Just Smile

When times are tough just smile.
When you're feeling down just smile.
When you're scared or lonely just smile.
When you feel the whole world is against you just smile.
When someone puts you down just smile.
When I see your face I just smile.

Sarah Oakley (12)
Appleby Grammar School, Appleby

Tap The Key

Tap the key and hear the sound, play a tune and play it loud
The sound of the key is so gentle and soft
It makes me never want to stop
I learn new things all the time, pressing the keys up and down
There's never a limit to things I can learn when
It comes to the piano I'll be there
You don't want to play the key too soft
You need to play it powerfully enough
When playing the piano there are up to 4 beats in a bar
My heart pumps every time I hear the sound
The sound of the piano playing.

Hannah Larmour (12)
Appleby Grammar School, Appleby

It

It is a way of calming down after a hard day's work,
It can enthral me in an endless trance,
It echoes through my ears mesmerizing me for hours on end,
It feels like I'm playing in front of a thousand splendid souls,
It sings more sweetly than an angelic choir,
It smells like an autumnal fantasy forest,
It is an entertaining stooge that's been loved beyond measure,
It is a magical and wondrous creation,
It is my guitar!

Olly Gutteridge [12]
Appleby Grammar School, Appleby

Paddy!

'Paddy!' I shout as he gallops along,
'Slow down wild thing!'
And he carries on.

We approach the jump, he pings it with ease,
He turns to the next,
Then jumps through the trees.

We're in the woods, it's dull and dark,
He breaks to trot,
As he hears a bark.

A dog runs out, he's off again,
He finishes the course,
I pat his messy mane.

He's out of breath, I am as well,
He should be tired,
But you can hardly tell!

We come back home with a red rosette,
He's finally calmed down,
After giving him his hay net.

Emma Addison (12)
Appleby Grammar School, Appleby

The Schoolyard Better

I enter the schoolyard looking for my better,
I spot him and he spots me.
'I'm not up to this; I should run,' I mutter,
Making the decision not to flee,
I face the boy and he faces me.

He stared me down with a smug smile,
His face is stone and his eyes like diamonds.
I pull out the puzzle with great style,
'Solve it then,' he demands with great violence.
I face the boy and he faces me.

I crackle the puzzle into place,
I am not hesitant to start and neither are his insults.
Harsh words and curses are rocks fired at my face,
I soak up these words like they're sponge bullet assaults.
I face the boy and he faces me.

As I click everything into place he cannot believe his eyes,
He is still confident, he is in denial.
As I finish the puzzle the look on his face is one of surprise,
Now it's my turn to wear that smug smile.
I face the boy and he faces me.

'You cheated; you didn't solve that, no way,'
I look at him with an ear to ear smile.
'You cheated, I don't know how but you did, I won't pay,'
I don't care, I beat him and that was worthwhile.
I face the boy but he can't face me.

Robert Aldam (12)
Appleby Grammar School, Appleby

Bubble, Sizzle and Drip!

My popadom is crunchy and hard,
My pumpernickel is exactly like card,
My pasta is soft and chewy,
My pudding is limp and gooey.

My Doritos go crack and crunch,
My teeth go gobble and munch.
My chicken goes sizzle and bang,
My beef needs to hang and hang.

My Chinese is called sweet and sour,
My bread is made of self-raising flour.
My Indian is called chicken korma,
My vindaloo is a lot warmer.

My chocolate is just for men,
My stew will be ready by then.
My chewing gum got stuck in my hair,
My cheese needs to air.

My sister made up a new breakfast muffin,
But it wasn't as nice as the MacDonald's McMuffin,
My dad made a vindaloo,
And after we all needed the loo.

So finally we've come to the end,
I hope I haven't driven you around the bend,
But if I have eat some food,
And soon you'll be in the mood.

Holly Daldry (12)
Appleby Grammar School, Appleby

Her Smile

Her smile is made of diamonds,
Shiny and attractive,
Her hair is made of silk,
Soft and smooth,
Her eyes are made of jewels,
Twinkling and wide,
Her lips are made of cushions,
Comforting and rosy,
Her arms are made of angel's wings,
Graceful and silky,
Her hands are made of velvet,
Fluffy and loving,
Her heart is made of gold
And that's what matters to me.

Alice Shaw (12)
Appleby Grammar School, Appleby

Share

When you need a friend for advice
A friend to ask 'Do I look OK'?
A friend to say 'You look nice'
You will look no other way.

Texting, laughing, that's all we do
Laughing until we cry
I have so much fun with you
Will be laughing until we die

Memories like gold for us
I know I can trust you forever
Sharing secrets about us
Fall out? Never.

Mollie Ratcliffe (13)
Appleby Grammar School, Appleby

Winter Ride

Walking down the cold and frosty lane
Lifting up the old, rusty chain
I can see him in the field ahead, he looks at me and tosses his head.

He gallops over to say hello, because it's time to go
We start our ride down the lane, frost settling on his wirey mane
Losing ourselves, and enjoying our ride
We canter on home, feeling warm inside, both treasuring our
Winter ride.

Molly Sellars (12)
Appleby Grammar School, Appleby

Dance . . .

A bird in flight,
On a cold, dark night,
Twinkles in their eyes,
Graceful as butterflies.
Pirouetting, spiralling as free as air,
Spinning, people's destiny,
The smell of cheap hairspray,
Costumes glitter like fish scales.

All as one,
Line in line,
Dancing to the ballet song,
Free as the tide,

Gliding along,
Living the song,
As time goes by,
Graceful, elegant, beautiful,
All like one.

Hope Matthews [12]
Appleby Grammar School, Appleby

What A Ride

When I'm on a roller coaster,
Is the time I feel most free,

Going so fast I can barely breathe,
It's such a thrill for me.

At first the long climb, so steep, so high,
I feel so brave, so excited, almost touching the sky,

The highest point of the Pepsi Max was such a thrill,
My best ever roller coaster ride until,

The Kumali at Flamingo Land on holiday last year,
An experience so brilliant I wanted to cheer.

Once strapped in my seat, I knew it was worth the wait,
Whizzing round corners, upside down, it was great,

There's only one trouble with these rides I reckon,
Stand in line for ages then it's over in seconds.

Tom Silverwood Simpson (12)
Appleby Grammar School, Appleby

Shopping With A Friend

Shopping with a friend is cool
There's nothing forbidden, no rule
And no parents to say what's suitable
Or to tell you what's unaffordable,
Actually you don't need to be rich
To try on whatever your eyes wish.

Shopping with a friend is so nice
You might forget budget and pride
And buy things you don't need
Just by habit, not by greed
Like get ten or eleven similar tops
From two or three different shops.

Ellen Cannon (12)
Appleby Grammar School, Appleby

1944

I strolled along the beach in 1944,
Armed with a rifle,
Knocking at death's door
I took it out and shot, 50 men at least,
The pile of corpses, roses like yeast,
However, it was to end happily,
That despite all the dead,
And all the bloodshed,
It was the end
He had won
But then suddenly, I dropped my gun
I looked down,
To see blood oozing from the blood gown.
I slumped to the floor, crippled in pain,
But at least I had not fought in vain
My story is complete
My tale ends here
I lived and died, knowing no fear.
But now I was dead
After all the bloodshed
But at least, we won in the end . . .

Matthew Davidson (12)
Appleby Grammar School, Appleby

The Oval Game

Rugby, a wonderful game,
Which can lead to great fame.
A master of skills,
That provide all the thrills.
To run, pass and kick,
Through players like bricks.
Head for the line,
And score the greatest try of mine.
Next task in hand,
Convert to the land.
The team roars like lions,
As we go six up against the Syons.
One minute to go,
Everything I throw.
But they break the line,
As they score from their number nine.
It all comes down to the final kick,
Which will decide which way the points tick.

Heart and soul to this wonderful game.

The oval game

Josh Addison-Adams [12]
Appleby Grammar School, Appleby

What Matters To Me . . .

So what matters to me?
My very loving family,
They are ever so kind,
I love them all the time,
And that's what matters to me.

My friends are the best
Better than the rest.
They all come very close,
To my great family
What would I do without my family?
And that's what matters to me.

I can't think of anything else,
But these two above,
Because nothing matches,
What they mean to me,
They are all so special,
I can't put it into words,
And that's what matters to me.

Chloe Robinson (12)
Appleby Grammar School, Appleby

Lazy

Everyone loves a lazy day,
In your jimjams eating junk,
Where you don't have to do or say,
Anything you don't want.

Watching all your favourite channels,
With the dog snoring by the fire,
Being green using solar panels,
That's what I desire.

Shut the curtains, munching popcorn,
Eyes glaring at the square screen,
Staying awake until after dawn,
Watching scary films that make you scream!

At the end of the day you're all tired out,
After that *hard* task,
Tomorrow I'll be up and about,
Trick or treating, wearing a Halloween mask.

Jasmine Macleod (12)
Appleby Grammar School, Appleby

Life

I walk through the door
To hear the fire's roar.
To see my mum looking
In the recipe book for what she's cooking.
On my plate is a steamy casserole,
For dessert some creamy profiteroles.
I have a scrap with my brother,
Soon to be yelled at by my mother.
Now calm has come across the house,
You can't even hear my pet mouse.
I'm laid in bed
With a sleepy head.
Deep into a dream,
What more can be said?

Emma Bellas (13)
Appleby Grammar School, Appleby

A Poem About What I Love

I love it when I do dance.
I love it when I go to Blackpool Pleasure Beach.
I love it when I go out with my friends.
I love it when I play with my kitten.
I love it when I come to school.
I love it when the silky blue water comes to my feet.
I love it when I see the sun shines in the light blue sky.
I love it when I do dance with Miss McDellend.

Chloe Sanderson [13]
Ashton Community Science College, Ashton

A Poem About What I Love

I love it when sun shines like stars in the sky.
I love it when I go horse riding.
I love it when the silky blue sea comes to my feet.
I love it when I'm not at school.
I love it when I do dance with Miss McClelland.
I love it when the fish come up out of the water.
I love to go to Blackpool Pleasure Beach.
I love it when the sun shines in the spring-blue sky.

Rachael Martin (13)
Ashton Community Science College, Ashton

Things I Love

I love it when it snows on Christmas Day
I love it when a star glows on a clear blue sky
I love it when I grow
I love it when I get loads of presents every year
I love it when I am out with my mum
I love it when I get chocolate oh my gosh, yum!

Lindsay Hindle (13)
Ashton Community Science College, Ashton

Have A Spooky Halloween

Halloween is the time of year,
For witches, pumpkins and green witchy hair.
For all to laugh and be spooked,
Knocking on people's doors and shouting, 'Boo'!

Knock on a door and shout, 'Trick or treat',
Do you want some money or a little treat,
Once your pumpkin has been filled with goodies
Go back home and tip it all out
And then do it all again but this time *shout*, 'Trick or treat'.

Make sure you're not alone
But with all your mates
Or a wolf might use you as its bait.

Megan Dodds [11]
Belmont Comprehensive School, Durham

Halloween

As the darkness nears, the world fears what is ahead of the night.
The lightness of day is drained away and the world is filled with light.
The dark creatures begin to wake and roam the night sky.
Fear spreads among the clouds.
The witches are nearing, the pumpkins are out.
Streets are filled with excitement and joy as the children come out to play.
Skeletons, wolves, wizards and more join together this one special day.
Halloween!
Sweet wrappers and witches hats,
Dark sky, torches and scary masks,
Halloween is an unforgettable part of the year!
Spooky costumes we all display,
Who is best? They ask and pray,
Skeletons, wolves, wizards and more join together this one special day.
Halloween!

Sarah Cooke [12]
Belmont Comprehensive School, Durham

Halloween

When the moon went up on Halloween night,
Skeletons came out their damp graves,
The vampires came out for the midnight bite,
Monsters came out their dark caves,
Witches flew and blocked the moonlight,
Carved pumpkins' flames wave,
When the moon went down after Halloween night,
All was well and all was bright.

Caitlin McGranaghan (11)
Belmont Comprehensive School, Durham

Time To Shine

The crowd roaring like a lion,
As I step up the tunnel,
I'm in a new world now,
Football,
The whistle blows,
Action starts,
Crunching tackles dominate the game,
Until in the last seconds,
Free kick.
I have to keep my composure,
Boom!
Yes!
I'm a newborn hero,
This is my time to shine.

Lewis O'Connor (11)
Belmont Comprehensive School, Durham

My Grandad, John

My grandad was my best friend
He kept on fighting to the end.

He led a happy life
And had a beautiful wife

My grandad and his birds
He had them all in herds!

Alysha Robinson (11)
Belmont Comprehensive School, Durham

Medusa

M is for the mighty Medusa!
E is for the energy that she had a lot of!
D is for danger that she was full of!
U is for the underground tomb where she lived!
S is for the speed her slithering snakes gave!
A is for the accuracy that she had in her eyes!

Adam Warrilow (11)
Belmont Comprehensive School, Durham

The Shadows

I'm not the type of person you'd see interacting with others . . .
I like to hide in the shadows and under covers . . .
My shadows are my havens . . . they never leave my side . . .
If they ever left me I'm sure I would have cried . . .
I wasn't always like this, I was once normal . . .
But that soon faded and the human part of me also went away . . .
No one knows I exist . . . at least not anymore . . .
And I like it that way because I never get bored . . .
Don't feel bad for me, because I don't want your sympathy . . .
The world has deserted me . . . and I don't seem to care . . .
Because I can always count on my shadows . . .
And know they will be there . . .

Casie-Marie Shaba (12)
Belmont Comprehensive School, Durham

Trick Or Treat

Dressing up,
In costumes galore.
Buying them,
From Tesco's store.

Lots of sweets,
Feeling sick.
Toffees and chocolates,
Get the bowl quick!

Standing in the freezing cold,
Knocking from door to door.
Getting scared from pumpkins,
And blood and gore.

Vampires, ghosts and ghoulies,
Witches and black cats.
What's that noise?
Maybe it's bats!

Coming home at night,
Tired from all the walking.
Eating all your sweets,
While me and my friends are talking.

Katie Clifford (13) & Emily Holden(12)
Belmont Comprehensive School, Durham

Basilisk

The king of snakes hides away,
Away from light of day,
Day means roosters are awake,
Awake the basilisk is lethal,
Lethal venom in its fangs,
Fangs sharp as a needle point,
Point of the tail, snake-like and long,
Long is not the time you will have to live,
Live you will not if you look into its eyes,
Eyes provide danger,
Danger banished by phoenix,
Phoenix tears cure venom,
Venom kills easily,
Easily avoid the basilisk's stare,
Stare at the reflection and you're not dead,
Dead is the basilisk, if it hears the rooster's crow.

Bethany Steer (11)
Belmont Comprehensive School, Durham

The Minotaur

The Minotaur was a Cretan monster,
Kept within a fiendish puzzle,
A labyrinth was its home lair,
Built by Daedalus, it had no muzzle.

Half-man, half-bull, the Minotaur was,
Pasiphae its mam, she'd been had,
Tricked by Poseidon to fall in love,
With Minotaur offspring that was bad.

King Minotaur had an annual take,
Seven youths, seven maidens were the deal,
Sent into the Minotaur's lair,
Fourteen people, a very big meal.

The people could not take any more,
Their confidence was at zero,
Theseus with Ariadne's help killed the Minotaur,
And he became a big hero.

Robert Macdonald (11)
Belmont Comprehensive School, Durham

Manticore

M anticore, manticore, oh how dark you are,
A nd all evil that you do is as black as night.
N ow I say a poem of hate so strong,
T o the east and to the west all shall hear.
I think that as you swoop and soar that I will run in terror,
C os you are as strong as a rock.
O ther than that you are the most evil thing on this Earth,
R ight now when we are scared you kill all you see.
E vermore you are the terrifying creature.

Jacob Taylor [12]
Belmont Comprehensive School, Durham

Medusa

M is for mythical creature.
E is for her evil actions.
D is for her devious mind.
U is for her unbelievably ugly face.
S is for her stone turning charm.
A is for her aggressive behaviour.

Emma Ross (11)
Belmont Comprehensive School, Durham

Medusa

M is for monstrous,
E is for her emerald eyes,
D is for her dreadful breath,
U is for her ugly face,
S is for her snakes for hair,
A is for angriness at Perseus.

Josie Ng (11)
Belmont Comprehensive School, Durham

Bonfire And Fireworks

The crowd gather before it begins,
The sky is dark and the cold is unbearable,
The sparklers are lit, that give off some heat,
And then it begins.

All the colours of the rainbow,
Little kids cover their ears,
People 'wooo' and stare at the sky,
Different shapes excite the crowd.

The final fireworks are being lit,
Some people are starting to leave,
Waving their glowsticks to light the way,
All the crowd have left.

They are packed away,
But there are still people getting cut down prices,
They will need to be carried away
After the excitement of the day.

Luke Dury & Chris Armstrong (12)
Belmont Comprehensive School, Durham

Halloween

Getting dressed up for trick or treat
Ghosts, skeletons, witches and wizards
Haunted houses give you a scare
Screaming, shouting, it's not fair!

Treats and tricks for all
Chocolate, sweets, is what we want
Knock-knock at the door
'Trick or treat', is what they shout
And all the sweets are in their mouths!

Tricks are on the way
Hand in spaghetti and goo
Eating hot chocolate and a cold stew!

From start to finish it's all great
Halloween, what a great date!

Caitlin Owston (12) & Georgia Hirst (13)
Belmont Comprehensive School, Durham

Halloween Night

On the 31st night of the 10th month,
All night's creatures come out to play,
Life won't last forever,
But death is here to stay.

Such a misunderstood bunch,
Are the creatures of the night,
What can the dead do?
It's the alive that ought to fright.

And we all know that vampires,
Are only hopeless romantics,
And ghosts are bound to make you smile,
With gravity defiant antics!

So when that night comes around,
Please bear in mind,
That these people really are,
The sweetest souls you'll find!

Catherine Dent & Lucy McIlroy (12)
Belmont Comprehensive School, Durham

Infant Break

When the clock says half-past ten,
Playtime then begins.
Kids run to the playground!
And then there's fuss and din.

Anna's pushing Lucas,
Into the water trough.
Meredith shows her swinging skills
But very soon gets off.

Mark is sliding down the slide,
But falls and bumps his head.
Celestina's thinking that it's
Really full of dread.

Isadora's throwing sand,
And Susan falls asleep.
Caleb's playing shepherd,
Luna is the sheep.

Alejandro's bragging he's the
Best at hide-and-seek.
Lucy's standing in the corner,
Small and quiet and meek.

Xylie's climbing ladders,
Kat watches far below.
Alistair thinks he'll play a trick
And pulls out Xylie's bow.

Melanie's on the trampoline,
Paice says he wants a go.
That he wants to get on too,
But Qai is saying no.

Violet goes inside a while,
And comes out with a snack.
But soon discovers her friend Rose
Has been whispering behind her back.

Sunny and Grace are laughing,
Carlos hits them with the rake.
What a lot of racket,
During
    Infants
        Break.

Bethany Hitchen (12)
Belmont Comprehensive School, Durham

Fireworks In The Sky

Oh a cold, chilled night,
The wind whistles in the air,
Sends shivers through you,
Looking up at the sky . . . waiting for something to happen.

Bang! Bang! Fireworks explode!
Colour bursting in the sky,
Blue, red, orange colours galore,
You don't know where to look.

As the fireworks die,
And fade into the sky,
The colour disappears,
And the black takes over.

Back to the beginning,
The show is over,
Time to go home,
On a brilliant evening.

Jack Wilkie (12)
Belmont Comprehensive School, Durham

Welcome To My World

Flashing lights,
Paparazzi,
Waiting to take,
A picture of me!

Film today,
Film tomorrow,
Busy all week,
That's just me!

Centre stage,
A single spotlight,
Shining,
To put me in the light!

Screaming fans,
Anywhere I go,
What can I say?
My life's a show!

I am a celeb,
As you can see,
So come live a day,
In the life of me!

Love to be famous?
Love to be me?
That's too bad,
Cause you will never be me!

Gemma Ross (13)
Belmont Comprehensive School, Durham

Halloween Night

Can you remember Halloween Night,
When people at the door,
Gave you
A great big fright.

The scary masks
And the great big googly eyes,
Looking for someone
To surprise.

Thomas David Lee (11)
Belmont Comprehensive School, Durham

The Cyber Bullying Poem!

The texts I receive from people
I once trusted, torture my mind,
And soon I will give up!
I feel like a stranger that people abandoned.

The words that I receive are cruel,
I wish I could cry in front of my mum.
But the problem is I am scared to tell the truth.

I know that when I sign into Facebook,
The messages are waiting!
I feel I was distraught!
I feel unloved!
I feel angry!
When will it stop?

Ellie Weatherburn (11)
Belmont Comprehensive School, Durham

The Bullying Poem

When I went to school, Mum, I remembered what you said,
Not to be with the bad ones
As they might put thoughts in my head.
Later that night, I went to bed,
Kept on thinking what those bullies said.
I tossed and turned all night long
Couldn't stop thinking what's going on.
I used to stand out and be loud
But now I feel like I blend in with the crowd.

Emma Colledge (11)
Belmont Comprehensive School, Durham

Halloween

H is for horror films
A is for apple dunking
L is for lanterns
L is for liquorice
O is for October
W is for witches
E is for evil spirits
E is for eerie devils
N is for naughty tricks.

Samantha Davison (11)
Belmont Comprehensive School, Durham

Doomsday

Doomsday's round the corner,
Happiness is falling smaller,
The winter's night,
Will bring a fright,
Of tales never foretold.

When the clock strikes six,
You must light the wicks,
It's time for tricks,
And less for treats,
Are you ready . . . here they come!

When the next clock ticks,
It means pick and mix,
Have a family bet,
Who gets the most ket,
The tales are now foretold.

Pumpkin men,
And frightful fire,
All we need is a fearsome choir,
Doomsday's here,
So careful now,
The night has now begun!

Philip Andrew Smith (11) & Daniel Andrew Appleby (12)
Belmont Comprehensive School, Durham

My Home

There's a place in my home
Where nobody likes except me.
My home is my place to be,
It means nothing to you but the world to me.
It's full of all my things,
Where my precious things are kept,
Where all my adventures take place,
A jungle, a kingdom or even a flooded city swept.
This place is my home.
It's never to be seen by anyone, except me.

Toni Carina Adams (11)
Lord Lawson of Beamish School, Chester le Street

Home

Seeing my mam in the house when I come home from school
When I take off my coat, at 8 o'clock I fight for the remote
The home is where my pets are
My home is a place of love and happiness
Before I go to bed I have a warm glass of milk.

Molly Adamson (11)
Lord Lawson of Beamish School, Chester le Street

My Home

My home is my place
My bedroom is a quiet place
My living room is a noisy place
My dining room is a cooking place

In my house there is a room
A sporty room, a gaming room
A sleeping room
A relaxing room

In my house
There is an animal room
A reading room
And my private room.

Daniel Austin (11)
Lord Lawson of Beamish School, Chester le Street

Home Sweet Home

Home sweet home
Home sweet home
I'll tell you a poem about my
Home sweet home

I live in my bedroom
Which is pink and blue inside
Cupboards in the corners
My bed at the far side

Home sweet home
Home sweet home
I'll do the next part of my poem
About my home sweet home

Cosy and comfy
Safe and sound
Time to relax
So come on round!
Cooking in the kitchen
Playing with the pets
While my mam's cooking fish fingers
And potato croquets

Home sweet home
Home sweet home
I've now finished my poem
About my home sweet home.

Hannah Beck (11)
Lord Lawson of Beamish School, Chester le Street

My Home

A house in Birtley is my home
Calm and quiet describes my home
My bedroom is my favourite place
A comfortable home, a family home, my home

Local services just around the corner
Good choice of television and radio (BBC North East and Cumbria)
3D cinema just nearby! (The Metro Centre)
My area, my suburb, my home

There are some negatives
Noisy neighbours, a bus (the M2 and the M3) every 10 minutes!
However, I can live with it
Easy transport, the local area! My home

That's my area; everything I need is in the area
So come down to Birtley in County Durham
Or nearby Gateshead and Newcastle upon Tyne
Or even Sunderland!
My region, the North East, my Birtley, my home.

Casey Bell (12)
Lord Lawson of Beamish School, Chester le Street

My Home

I love to be at home
Playing with my brother
Kicking a football with my dad
Baking cookies with my mother

Playing in the garden on my trampoline
Backdrops, seatdrops, flips and a lot more
I love watching films in my cosy home
But I don't like watching films with gore

My home is a happy place
There's nowhere else I would rather be
Laughter, family and love all combined
Makes my home a special place for me.

Shay-Rebecca Bennison (11)
Lord Lawson of Beamish School, Chester le Street

My Home Is . . .

My home is full of active
Friends and family

My home is as lively
A lion catching its prey

My home is cosy
Like a big, cuddly teddy bear

My home has a loving, big, caring room.
My home is where I love to eat.
My home is where I love to sleep.

My home is where I love to chill out
With all of my friends.

Lauren Bradley (11)
Lord Lawson of Beamish School, Chester le Street

This Is My Home

This is my home
Which I live in with my family
And I live here quite happily.

This is my room
Which is baby-pink
It's a lovely place to sit and think.

This is the kitchen
Which is like my brother's playroom
Where he draws the stars and moon.

This is the living room
Where the computer is
Where I drink my Fanta fizz.

Then there's the bathroom
Where I have a bubble bath
Sometimes I count the bubbles like I'm in maths.

This is my home
Where I live with my family
And I live here happily.

Caitlin Bramwell (11)
Lord Lawson of Beamish School, Chester le Street

War

All across no-man's land
There's a chilling haze ahead
We are fighting on the sand
Everyone is dead

There's blood and guts all over
I don't know what to do
What's that? *Bombs!* Take cover
I want this to be through.

I can't take this anymore
I think I'm going to die
I can feel myself at death's door
If only I could fly!

Daniel Charles (13)
Lord Lawson of Beamish School, Chester le Street

Home?

What do we mean by the word home?
Is it a place where we go to be alone?
Or a place where we go to be surrounded
By love, noise, havoc and chaos?
Is it a place that only we know,
Or a place that is open for all to see?
A warm or cold, unusual place,
For only you and me,
No one knows the meaning -
Does it have one at all?
I guess it is just what we want it to be
And to visit, all we must do is call.

Natasha Cox (14)
Lord Lawson of Beamish School, Chester le Street

My Room

My room is a place to go
A place to go when I am angry or upset
A place to keep
A place to care for
A place to respect and keep tidy
A place to relax
A place to watch your favourite programme
A place to work
A place to have a sleepover
A place to settle down
A place to sleep.

Molly Cronnie (11)
Lord Lawson of Beamish School, Chester le Street

My Home Is . . .

My home is where I'm loved
My home is where I'm bugged

My family is active and playful
My family is sometimes hateful

My house is where I play
My house is where I have my say

My home is where I like to eat
My home is where I like to sleep

My home is open for all my friends
We all used to make lots of dens

But when I come home and open the door
I notice that I love it so.

Rebecca Cryer (11)
Lord Lawson of Beamish School, Chester le Street

My Home Is . . .

My home is where I sleep at night
My home is where my mam gets a fright
My home is where I talk during the night
My home is where I normally get a fright
My home is where I play out at night
My home is where bacon sandwiches are made
My home is where my tea is made
My home is where my breakfast is made
My home is a loving and caring home
My home is where laughter and enjoyment is made.

I love my home!

Courtney Dixon (11)
Lord Lawson of Beamish School, Chester le Street

Home

H ome is a happy place where you live
O ur house is special because without it we would be living on the streets
M y family live with me
E njoying it every second.

Tommy Edwards (11)
Lord Lawson of Beamish School, Chester le Street

War

It's early in the morning,
I hear my mates moaning and groaning,
I'm wondering if I'm going to make it,
Everyone's saying they can't take it.

I wish I was at home,
I'm standing here like a garden gnome.
Bombs exploding everywhere,
I don't know why I'm here, it's just not fair.

I look around, blood, bodies, that's all I see,
I hope that's not going to be me.
My dead body, that's what my mate will see.

Teri Glasgow (13)
Lord Lawson of Beamish School, Chester le Street

My House

A warm glass of milk or a hot cup of tea,
When I get home my family comfort me!

Tucked up in bed so comfy and warm,
The shelter above keeps out the storm!

The lovely smell of the Sunday roast,
Oh no! One of the Yorkshire puddings has gone,
It must have been a ghost!

At 7 o'clock we watch the TV,
We all enjoy it, Mum, Dad and me!

Every morning I wake up to see a dove,
A house is not a home without love!

Ruby Glendinning (11)
Lord Lawson of Beamish School, Chester le Street

War

I sit there,
I sit and I listen,
Why don't I fight?
Am I not brave?

I sit there,
Frightened! Frozen! Petrified!
Frozen at the thought of death.

Bang! Crash! Scream!
Ringing in my ears.
Another bombshell.

I sit there cold as stone,
As the angry rifles click and clatter.
All of a sudden the sky roars,
Tap, tap, the rain on my helmet.

I sit there wet and cold,
Clutching my rifle.
I am waiting,
Waiting for what?

I stand,
Maybe a sharp shooter will pick me off.
But instead, silence strikes,
A whistle blows.

My blood runs cold.
Two seconds ago I wanted to die,
But not now.
I want to live.

Dominic Gowland [13]
Lord Lawson of Beamish School, Chester le Street

It Doesn't Matter At All

Your house is big,
And mine is small,
But it doesn't matter at all.

You come in,
And I go out.

Your house is big,
And mine is small,
But it doesn't matter at all.

You go up,
And I go down.

Your house is big,
And mine is small,
But it doesn't matter at all.

Your house is like a desert big with space,
Mine is like a dog's kennel, small and cosy.

You love your house,
And I love mine.

Your house is big,
And mine is small,
But it doesn't matter at all.

You have your home,
And I have mine.
It doesn't matter how big or small,
We all have our own,
It doesn't matter what they are like.

Samantha Turnbull (12)
Lord Lawson of Beamish School, Chester le Street

My Home Is . . .

My home is where I live
My home is where I keep my pets
My home is where I store my food
My home is snug and warm
My home is where I blast my music
My home is where I watch TV and films
My home is where I play my PS3
My home is where I'm loved
My home is where I sleep
My home is sometimes quiet
My home is where I keep warm
My home is where I have fun.

Dylan Urwin (11)
Lord Lawson of Beamish School, Chester le Street

Home

Home is a special place
In the washer room it is cold like an ice cream cone.
While my dog stays at home, she likes to chew on her juicy bone.
As you come through the door, the cat steps on your toes
And when you come in my room, my teddies sit in rows.
When you're in the garden,
Felix, the cat across the road, comes to say hello.
He always keeps me company, he'll never leave me alone.
When my dad plays the keyboard, he knows the right tone,
While the guinea pig eats his tea, after he'll sit on your knee.
Of course the dog gets in her jealous mode,
She'll come and sit with us too.
On the lawn where my cat sits, she meets her friend and starts to play.
I now can't wait for the next day.
I love my home.

Jasmine Whittle (11)
Lord Lawson of Beamish School, Chester le Street

Home

Home is where the heart is,
It is the place to be,
With home comforts around you
And a caring family!

There is no place quite like it,
It's my safest place to be,
A home that is so full of love
And it means the world to me.

Home is sweet and sour,
As we go through good and bad,
Sometimes being hectic,
Yes, it really can get mad!

For all there are the mad times,
There are the great times too,
Home sweet home, it is the best,
A special place for you.

Taylor Wilson (11)
Lord Lawson of Beamish School, Chester le Street

Home Sweet Home

H uge home
O dd home
M essy home
E co home

S aturday morning home
W inter home
E verlasting home
E T go home
T en out of ten home

H ilarious home
O pening home
M arvellous home
E nd of home.

Harry Young (11)
Lord Lawson of Beamish School, Chester le Street

Home Sweet Home

H appy days.
O pen doors for all my friends and family.
M emories that will live forever.
E veryone for Christmas.

S ounds of love and laughter.
W ith all the family.
E ach day different and
E very day new.
T ime to eat around the table.

H ome in the winter with the warm log fire.
O ranges in the fruit bowl.
M mm, the smell of dinner.
E motions are shared.

Lauren Boll (11)
Lord Lawson of Beamish School, Chester le Street

A Special Place

My home is a special place,
My place.
I play, read, have fun, laugh,
Have arguments and live in my home.
I love to hang out in my bedroom,
To just relax and have time to think.
My house is noisy and loud,
But I wouldn't want it any other way.
When I am in my house,
I always feel warm and cosy,
I feel safe.
My home is a special place,
My place.

Bethany Melvin (12)
Lord Lawson of Beamish School, Chester le Street

Home

Come in and we will respect you
There is nothing to be scared of
It is warm and welcoming to all
You can sit and do nothing all day, every week
And it will still always love you.

Cameron Mitchell (11)
Lord Lawson of Beamish School, Chester le Street

My Home

I feel safe in my home because all my family are with me.
My dream bedroom would have a walk-in wardrobe, just for me.
When my mam does the ironing, it makes me mad because I have to put it away.
All about me, my room has everything I need in it.
All for me, my bedroom is a place for privacy.
Only for me, I would like to make my living room more comfy with lots of books.
Just for me, these are all the things I love about my home
And this is all about me.

Abbie Oldroyd (11)
Lord Lawson of Beamish School, Chester le Street

Home

Home is where you have some fights
And a couple of frights.
Home is where I have my evening bath
And maybe a giggle and a laugh.
Home is somewhere I go to sleep
And then have a real big treat!
My home means the world to me
Even without my lovely cup of tea.
Home is where my family are
Even when we argue a little bit more.
Home has the memories of you from little to big.
Home is somewhere you live.

Chelsea-Louise Quinn (11)
Lord Lawson of Beamish School, Chester le Street

Home Sweet Home

I eat food,
While jumping in my bed alone.
After that I play on my phone.
The time to clean the house,
After that I'm tired and moaning.
Then I am back in bed
With my earphones plugged in my head.
My home means the world to me,
Even when messy.
It's where I should be.
My home is the only one to me.

Humza Pervaiz (11)
Lord Lawson of Beamish School, Chester le Street

Featured Poets:
DEAD POETS
AKA Mark Grist & MC Mixy

Mark Grist and MC Mixy joined forces to become the 'Dead Poets' in 2008.

Since then Mark and Mixy have been challenging the preconceptions of poetry and hip hop across the country. As 'Dead Poets', they have performed in venues ranging from nightclubs to secondary schools; from festivals to formal dinners. They've appeared on Radio 6 Live with Steve Merchant, they've been on a national tour with Phrased and Confused and debuted their show at the 2010 Edinburgh Fringe, which was a huge success.

Both Mark and Mixy work on solo projects as well as working together as the 'Dead Poets'. Both have been Peterborough's Poet Laureate, with Mixy holding the title for 2010.

Tho 'Dead Poets' are available for workshops in your school as well as other events. Visit www.deadpoetry.co.uk for further information and to contact the guys!

Read on to pick up some fab writing tips!

Your
WORKSHOPS

In these Workshops We are going to look at writing styles and examine some literary techniques that the 'Dead Poets' use. Grab a pen, and let's go!

Rhythm Workshop

Rhythm in writing is like the beat in music. Rhythm is when certain words are produced more forcefully than others, and may be held for longer duration. The repetition of a pattern is what produces a 'rhythmic effect'. The word rhythm comes from the Greek meaning of 'measured motion'.

Count the number of syllables in your name. Then count the number of syllables in the following line, which you write in your notepad: 'My horse, my horse, will not eat grass'.

Now, highlight the longer sounding syllables and then the shorter sounding syllables in a different colour.

Di dum, di dum, di dum, di dum is a good way of summing this up.

You should then try to write your own lines that match this rhythm. You have one minute to see how many you can write!

Examples include:
'My cheese smells bad because it's hot' and
'I do not like to write in rhyme'.

For your poem, why don't you try to play with the rhythm? Use only longer beats or shorter beats? Create your own beat and write your lines to this?

Did you know ... ?

Did you know that paper was invented in China around 105AD by Ts'ai Lun. The first English paper mill didn't open until 1590 and was in Dartford.

Rhyme Workshop

Start off with the phrase 'I'd rather be silver than gold' in your notepad. and see if you can come up with lines that rhyme with it -

'I'd rather have hair than be bald'
'I'd rather be young than be old'
'I'd rather be hot than cold'
'I'd rather be bought than sold'

Also, pick one of these words and see how many rhymes you can find:

Rose

Wall

Warm

Danger

What kinds of rhymes did you come up with? Are there differences in rhymes? Do some words rhyme more cleanly than others? Which do you prefer and why?

Onomatopoeia Workshop

Divide a sheet of A4 paper into 8 squares.

You then have thirty seconds to draw/write what could make the following sounds:

Splash	Ping
Drip	Bang
Rip	Croak
Crack	Splash

Now try writing your own ideas of onomatopoeia Why might a writer include onomatopoeia in their writing?

Lists Workshop

Game - you (and you can ask your friends or family too) to write as many reasons as possible for the following topics:

Annoying things about siblings

The worst pets ever

The most disgusting ingredients for a soup you can think of

Why not try writing a poem with the same first 2, 3 or 4 words?

I am ...

Or

I love it when ...

Eg:

I am a brother

I am a listener

I am a collector of secrets

I am a messer of bedrooms.

Repetition Workshop

Come up with a list of words/ phrases, aim for at least 5. You now must include one of these words in your piece at least 6 times. You aren't allowed to place these words/ phrases at the beginning of any of the lines.

Suggested words/phrases:

Why

Freedom

Laughing

That was the best day ever

I can't find the door

I'm in trouble again

The best

Workshop
POETRY 101

Below is a poem written especially for Poetry Matters, by MC Mixy.
Why not try and write some more poems of your own?

What is Matter?

© MC Mixy

What matters to me may not be the same things that matter to you
You may not agree with my opinion mentality or attitude
The order in which I line up my priorities to move
Choose to include my view and do what I do due to my mood
And state of mind
I make the time to place the lines on stacks of paper and binds
Concentrate on my artwork hard I can't just pass and scrape behind
Always keep close mates of mine that make things right
And even those who can't … just cos I love the way they can try
What matters to me is doing things the right way
It's tough this game of life we play what we think might stray from what
others might say
In this world of individuality we all wanna bring originality
Live life and drift through casually but the vicious reality is
Creativity is unique
Opinions will always differ but if you figure you know the truth, speak
So many things matter to me depending on how tragically deep you wanna
go
I know I need to defy gravity on this balance beam
As I laugh and breathe draft and read map the scene practise piece smash
the beat and graphic release
Visual and vocal it's a standard procedure
Have to believe and don't bite the hand when it feeds ya

If you wanna be a leader you need to stay out of the pen where the sheep
are
The things that matter to me are
My art and my friends
That will stay from the start to the end
People will do things you find hard to amend
Expect the attacks and prepare you gotta be smart to defend
I put my whole heart in the blend the mass is halved yet again
I'm marked by my pen a big fish fighting sharks of men
In a small pond
Dodging harpoons and nets hooks and predators tryna dismember ya
I won't let them I won't get disheartened I can fend for myself
As long as I'm doing what's important
I'm my mind where I'm supported is a just cause to be supporting
In these appalling hard times I often find myself falling when
Only two aspects of my life keep me sane and allow me to stand tall again
Out of all of them two is a small number
It's a reminder I remind ya to hold necessity and let luxury fall under
Try to avoid letting depression seep through
Take the lesson we actually need a lot less than we think we do
So what matters to you?
They may be similar to things that matter to me
I'm actually lacking the need of things I feel would help me to succeed
Though I like to keep it simple, I wanna love, I wanna breed
I'm one of many individuals in this world where importance fluctuates and
varies
Things that matter will come and go
But the ones that stay for long enough must be worth keeping close
If you're not sure now don't watch it you'll know when you need to know
Me, I think I know now … yet I feel and fear I don't.

Turn overleaf for a poem by Mark Grist and some fantastic hints and tips!

Workshop
POETRY 101

What Tie Should I Wear Today?

© Mark Grist

I wish I had a tie that was suave and silk and slick,
One with flair, that's debonair and would enchant with just one flick,
Yeah, I'd like that … a tie that's hypnotizing,
I'd be very restrained and avoid womanising,
But all the lady teachers would still say 'Mr Grist your tie's so charming!'
As I cruise into their classrooms with it striking and disarming.
At parents' evenings my tie's charm would suffice,
In getting mums to whisper as they leave 'Your English teacher seems nice!'

Or maybe an evil-looking tie - one that's the business,
Where students will go 'Watch out! Mr Grist is
on the prowl with that evil tie.'
The one that cornered Josh and then ripped out his eye.
Yeah no one ever whispers, no one ever sniggers,
Or my tie would rear up and you'd wet your knickers.
Maybe one girl just hasn't heard the warning,
Cos she overslept and turned up late to school that morning,
And so I'd catch her in my lesson yawning … oh dear.
I'd try to calm it down, but this tie's got bad ideas.
It'd size the girl up and then just as she fears,
Dive in like a serpent snapping at her ears.
There'd be a scream, some blood and lots and lots of tears,
And she wouldn't be able to yawn again for years.

Or maybe … a tie that everyone agrees is mighty fine
And people travel from miles around to gawp at the design
I'd like that … a tie that pushes the boundaries of tieware right up to the limit
It'd make emos wipe their tears away while chavs say 'It's wicked innit?'
and footy lads would stop me with 'I'd wear that if I ever won the cup.'
And I'd walk through Peterborough to slapped backs, high fives, thumbs up
While monosyllabic teenagers would just stand there going 'Yup.'

I don't know. I'd never be sure which of the three to try
As any decision between them would always end a tie.

Tips and Advice for PERFORMING Your Poem

So you've written your poem, now how about performing it.
Whether you read your poem for the first time in front of your class, school or strangers at an open mic event or poetry slam, these tips will help you make the best of your performance.

Breathe and try to relax.

Every poet that reads in front of people for the first time feels a bit nervous, when you're there you are in charge and nothing serious can go wrong.

People at poetry slams or readings are there to support the poets. They really are!

If you can learn your poem off by heart that is brilliant, however having a piece of paper or notebook with your work in is fine, though try not to hide behind these.

It's better to get some eye contact with the audience.
If you're nervous find a friendly face to focus on.

Try to read slowly and clearly and enjoy your time in the spotlight.

Don't rush up to the microphone, make sure it's at the right height for you and if you need it adjusted ask one of the team around you.

Before you start, stand up as straight as you can and get your body as comfortable as you can and remember to hold your head up.

The microphone can only amplify what what's spoken into it; if you're very loud you might end up deafening people and if you only whisper or stand too far away you won't be heard.

When you say something before your poem, whether that's hello or just the title of your poem, try and have a listen to how loud you sound. If you're too quiet move closer to the microphone, if you're too loud move back a bit.

Remember to breathe! Don't try to say your poem so quickly you can't find time to catch your breath.

And finally, **enjoy!**

Poetry FACTS

Here are a selection of fascinating poetry facts!

No word in the English language rhymes with 'MONTH'.

William Shakespeare was born on 23rd April 1564 and died on 23rd April 1616.

The haiku is one of the shortest forms of poetic writing.
Originating in Japan, a haiku poem is only seventeen syllables, typically broken down into three lines of five, seven and five syllables respectively.

The motto of the Globe Theatre was 'totus mundus agit histrionem' [the whole world is a playhouse].

The Children's Laureate award was an idea by Ted Hughes and Michael Morpurgo.

The 25th January each year is Burns' Night, an occasion in honour of Scotland's national poet Robert Burns.

Spike Milligan's 'On the Ning Nang Nong' was voted the UK's favourite comic poem in 1998.

Did you know *onomatopoeia* means the word you use sounds like the word you are describing – like the rain *pitter-patters* or the snow *crunches* under my foot.

'Go' is the shortest complete sentence in the English language.

Did you know rhymes were used in olden days to help people remember the news? Ring-o'-roses is about the Plague!

The Nursery Rhyme 'Old King Cole' is based on a real king and a real historical event. King Cole is supposed to have been an actual monarch of Britain who ruled around 200 A.D.

Edward Lear popularised the limerick with his poem 'The Owl and the Pussy-Cat'.

Lewis Carroll's poem 'The Jabberwocky' is written in nonsense style.

POEM – noun

1. a composition in verse, esp. one that is characterized by a highly developed artistic form and by the use of heightened language and rhythm to express an intensely imaginative interpretation of the subject.

Poetry TIPS

We have compiled some helpful tips for you budding poets...

In order to write poetry, read lots of poetry!

Keep a notebook with you at all times so you can write whenever (and wherever) inspiration strikes.

Every line of a poem should be important to the poem and interesting to read. A poem with only 3 great lines should be 3 lines long.

Use an online rhyming dictionary to improve your vocabulary.

Use free workshops and help sheets to learn new poetry styles.

Experiment with visual patterns - does your written poetry create a good pattern on the page?

Try to create pictures in the reader's mind - aim to fire the imagination.

Develop your voice. Become comfortable with how you write.

Listen to criticism, and try to learn from it, but don't live or die by it.

Say what you want to say, let the reader decide what it means.

Notice what makes other's poetry memorable. Capture it, mix it up and make it your own. (Don't copy other's work word for word!)

Go wild. Be funny. Be serious. Be whatever you want!

Grab hold of something you feel - anything you feel - and write it.

The more you write, the more you develop. Write poetry often.

Use your imagination, your own way of seeing.

Feel free to write a bad poem, it will develop your 'voice'.

Did you know ...?

'The Epic of Gilgamesh' was written thousands of years ago in Mesopotamia and is the oldest poem on record.

Wordsmith

The *premier* magazine
for creative young people

A platform for your imagination and creativity. Showcase your ideas and have your say. Welcome to a place where like-minded young people express their personalities and individuality knows no limits.

For further information visit ***www.youngwriters.co.uk***.

A peek into Wordsmith world ...

Poetry and Short Stories

We feature both themed and non-themed work every issue. Previous themes have included; dreams and aspirations, superhero stories and ghostly tales.

Next Generation Author

This section devotes two whole pages to one of our readers' work. The perfect place to showcase a selection of your poems, stories or both!

Guest Author Features & Workshops

Interesting and informative tutorials on different styles of poetry and creative writing. Famous authors and illustrators share their advice with us on how to create gripping stories and magical picturebooks. Novelists like Michael Morpurgo and Celia Rees go under the spotlight to answer our questions.

The fun doesn't stop there ...

Every issue we tell you what events are coming up across the country. We keep you up to date with the latest film and book releases and we feature some yummy recipes to help feed the brain and get the creative juices flowing.

So with all this and more, Wordsmith is *the* magazine to be reading.

If you are too young for Wordsmith magazine or have a younger friend who enjoys creative writing, then check out Scribbler!. Scribbler! is for 7-11 year-olds and is jam-packed full of brilliant features, young writers' work, competitions and interviews too. For further information check out ***www.youngwriters.co.uk*** or ask an adult to call us on (01733) 890066.

To get an adult to subscribe to either magazine for you, ask them to visit the website or give us a call.

Home

H ome is where the heart is
O pen and warm
M erry and happy
E xciting and cheerful, it's always there for me.

Rosie Plunkett (11)
Lord Lawson of Beamish School, Chester le Street

War

Bang! Bang! Bang!
I was suddenly all alone in agony.
Thick, grey, misty smoke filled the clear air.
Deadly bullets shot across the sky.
What am I doing here?

War is not a happy place to be,
Shells whistled across the sky.
A mass of bitter blood poured out of bodies.
The soldier was dead.

I ran and ran and ran!
Dodging soldiers and crawling
In the thick, deep, wet earth.

Louisa Preece (13)
Lord Lawson of Beamish School, Chester le Street

Home

H appy home is a happy life
O pen door
M emories that last a lifetime
E quivalent to a fantasy land.

Grace Prudhoe (11)
Lord Lawson of Beamish School, Chester le Street

My Home

My home has everything I need,
From bedrooms, computers and a couple of TVs!
My home is a place where I can be calm,
A place where I can come to no harm.

My home is where I can be relaxed,
Where I sit, read a book and just chillax!
I love my home, it's where I can be free . . .

My mam, my dad, my sister and me!

Lauren Ramshaw (12)
Lord Lawson of Beamish School, Chester le Street

My Home

My home is the place to be,
Where I can relax my mind and be calm and free.
There are rooms which I have explored which no one has seen,
Apart from me.

My bedroom is where I can live my fantasies and just be myself,
My living room is warm and cosy,
My garden is as fun as can be,
My home means absolutely everything to me.

Lucy Richardson (11)
Lord Lawson of Beamish School, Chester le Street

Welcome

W hether it's dark or light, cold or bright, you are always welcome.
E verybody in the family comes to visit, they are welcome.
L ots of aunties and uncles, parents and others, cousins and relations,
   sisters and brothers.
C ome and join in the fun, come, we welcome everyone.
O ver and over, year after year, we welcome our family.
M eet new arrivals, babies, young and free,
   family is what is important to me.
E verybody's welcome, family and friends, relationships are forever,
   they don't just end.

Kate Robinson (11)
Lord Lawson of Beamish School, Chester le Street

Home Inside

I have a room inside me,
It's full of happiness,
Warmth
And joy.

I have a room inside me,
I wish you could come along!

I have a room inside me,
It's full of love,
Laughter
And comfort.

I have a room inside me,
I wish you could come along!

Chloe Rose (11)
Lord Lawson of Beamish School, Chester le Street

War

As the air around me fills up with mustard gas,
Like a monster in the air,
I struggle, struggle to get the grimy, green gas mask on my face.
The poisonous gas wraps around me
With big hands of yellow, transparent fog.
I fear for my life as I stand still as the gas spreads around me,
I have nowhere to go.
I am as blind as a bat.
My friends are calling me like screaming hyenas.
I hear the gunshots around me, I panic so much,
I feel like I am alone in the worst nightmare
That you could ever think of.
The gunshots are getting closer, closer than before
And you can hear the bang and clang of each bullet.
I rush over to where I can hear my side of defence
Shouting at me.
We all hide in the trench from them.
I think we are nearly dead. Or are we?

Daniel Sanderson (13)
Lord Lawson of Beamish School, Chester le Street

Home

What is home to me?

Home to me is full of glee
Home to me is a laugh and a giggle
When I crawl into bed with a wriggle
Home is where I learnt to walk
As well as sing, dance and talk
Home is where I get into bed at night
As I snuggle under my duvet tight.

Hannah Sanderson (12)
Lord Lawson of Beamish School, Chester le Street

My Home

My home is where I hang my coat,
My home is where I have a thought,
But my home does not have a boat.
My home is where I sort my bedroom out.
My home is where my mum taught me.
My home is where chatter is in the air.
But my home is better than yours.
My home doesn't really matter,
But knock on my door.
You will see I have four.
Pick one
And be its core.

Jak Scott (11)
Lord Lawson of Beamish School, Chester le Street

Home Poem

H ome
O ven to cook
M oments to cherish
E very day it's yours

S afe
W here we eat, drink, live
E very night you go to sleep there
E very morning you wake up there
T ime to move on?

H appiness
O pen door at any time
M y life
E verlasting memory!

Lois Scott (11)
Lord Lawson of Beamish School, Chester le Street

My Home Is . . .

My house is really comfy.
My house is really tidy.
My house is where I play on my Xbox 360.
My house is really warm inside.
My house is really big, but my house is full of laughter.
My house has a really big garden.
My home is where they dance with me.
My home is where I live, but my house is really colourful.

Connor Shaw (11)
Lord Lawson of Beamish School, Chester le Street

Home Sweet Home

H appy home
O ld home
M ad home
E xploring home

S afe home
W eird home
E veryone welcome home
E xtremely cosy home
T eeming with life home

H opeful home
O utstanding home
M usical home
E xciting home

My home.

Jessica Simpson (11)
Lord Lawson of Beamish School, Chester le Street

Home Sweet Home!

H appy
O pen door at all times
M ore than comfortable
E fficient in every way

S anctuary
W onderful
E nchanting
E asy-going
T he place I love to live

H appy
O pen door at all times
M ore than comfortable
E fficient in every way.

Charlotte Smith (11)
Lord Lawson of Beamish School, Chester le Street

War's Conditions

Bodies strewn endlessly along the wide country meadows,
Crisp, white clouds mass over unforgiving skies,
Grass that was once green and luscious,
Now a rusty brown in the unforgiving sun

For life is all but well in the eyes of war and peace,
Of course, war isn't worth bullets, pain and suffering.
The millions of lives lost for their own cause,
Life in war is as bloody as gore.

The rose may blossom in the summertime orchard,
But a flower, not in sight, at least on battlefield planes.

Adam Soulsby (13)
Lord Lawson of Beamish School, Chester le Street

My Ideal Home

In the kitchen I would have,
A fridge that could hold all the king's feasts.
A hot chocolate machine fit for a beast.
In the games room I would have,
A 42″ plasma TV,
A super computer for my dog, BC.
In the garden I would have,
A meadow for my horses to graze,
A sunny spot for the sun to blaze.
In my bedroom I would have,
A music player for the latest beats,
A giant box for my favourite sweets.

Megan McIlwraith (11)
Lord Lawson of Beamish School, Chester le Street

My Home Is . . .

My home is where I sleep
My home is where I like the stuff I collect and keep
My home is where everyone eats every crumb
My home is where I laugh and play
My home is where nobody is born in May
My home is where I am loved
My home is where things move
My home is where I watch telly
My home is where nobody is smelly
My home is where my family are
My home is where my mam makes everything fair.

Chloe McLelland (11)
Lord Lawson of Beamish School, Chester le Street

My Home

My home is a noisy home.
My kitchen is small and I wish it was bigger.

My bedroom is my favourite room
Because I can do whatever I want
And keep all my stuff private.
It's also my favourite room
Because that is where I listen to music
And sing my own songs.

My dream room is a painting room
So I can paint all my favourite things
And whatever I want.

My living room is my cosy room
And that is where I play on my Nintendo Wii
And enjoy family time.
I also eat my tea and watch TV here.

Caitlin McAllister (12)
Lord Lawson of Beamish School, Chester le Street

Home Sweet Home!

H ome
O ven to cook
M arvellous life!
E ating nice meals

S miling family
W onderful
E very night I sleep here
E very morning I have my breakfast here
T he place that I love to live

H appy life
O utstanding home
M y life
E asy-going.

Georgia Maxwell (11)
Lord Lawson of Beamish School, Chester le Street

War

Another exhausting day in my nightmare
Yesterday starts again
I am already exhausted, as if I had run a marathon
Bang! Whistle! Swoosh!
As a death sentence nearly grabbed me
I thought my life was all over
How am I still alive?
My sweat dripped, dripped and dripped
It climbed down my petrified face.

I am a silent worm at war
Crawling through the thick and slick mud
Deep, deep down in the trench
Where the dead bodies smash and crash
Ending with a thud onto the gruesome floor
After they had been sniped silently.

Silence, silence and more silence
Is it all over?
Well, that's what I thought
Until zoom! Crackle!
The noises swept above me
I threw my head back to look up at the sky
I saw a shell of death swooping down towards me
Boom!
The bomb landed
This time it was all over
The lights went out
It turned into a dark, ghostly room
I couldn't see anything apart from pitch-black
A few minutes later which seemed like an hour
My eyes opened
But it was still dark
A beam of light pushed its way through the ash
I stood up and looked along the trench
Friendly soldiers were standing zombies
I looked down at the sleeping lions
They weren't breathing
The trench foot of a soldier caught my eye
It was ridiculous

It looked painful
I was shocked
A boil was like a curved Mount Everest
It was all over for that soldier . . .

A grenade flew towards me
I couldn't stop it
Boom!
That was the last I heard
It was definitely all over.

Daniel Martin (13)
Lord Lawson of Beamish School, Chester le Street

Home

When I am at home,
I feel like the king of Rome.
Without a doubt,
Home does not make me feel like a roundabout.

We live in a home,
Like a fish in a bowl.
It is a place where we can squeal
At the spiders that are real.

It is a place for a bee like me,
When I can sit and drink my cup of tea.
It is a place where I can slither and slide
Without people staring with their eyes open wide.

When I am at home,
I don't feel alone.
Now I must get to my dinner,
Before it is handled by a sinner.

Ayla Maddern (11)
Lord Lawson of Beamish School, Chester le Street

My Special Home

M agic home
Y our home

S uper home
P roud home
E xciting home
C razy home
I ncredible home
A mazing home
L oving home

H appy home
O ur home
M ad home
E veryone's home.

Catherine Lewins (11)
Lord Lawson of Beamish School, Chester le Street

My Home Is . . .

My home is a place where I like to chill.
My home is a great place.
My kitchen is a place where I like to cook.
My room could not be any better.
My home has got the best people in the world.
My kitchen feeds us every night.
My room lets me sleep every night.
My sitting room entertains my family.
My house is the gateway to Heaven.

Robbie Greenwell (11)
Lord Lawson of Beamish School, Chester le Street

My Home

Wake up in the morning
Go to bed at night
Go and come back from school
Have some food at night
Get my mum from work
Bring her home tonight
Make her food and water
And have the rest of the night
Come in and I will welcome you
To my lovely and warm home
Where we are a loving and welcoming home
We will love you and welcome you to my amazing home.

Charley Flynn (12)
Lord Lawson of Beamish School, Chester le Street

My Home

There's a room in my house where nobody goes,
It's a quiet and dark room,
A me and my pets room,
A keep out it's my room,
A safe, cosy, warm room,
My lovely, private room.

A tidy then messy room,
A listen to the top 40 room,
A get over with the homework room,
My own relaxing room.

Rebecca Harvison (11)
Lord Lawson of Beamish School, Chester le Street

Welcome Home

W e've missed you all so much
E very single day
L ife has been different
C ould you come and stay?
O n the icy doorstep we have waited
M orning and night
E ven through the ups and downs

H appiness made it right
O n the 3rd of January
M ornin' by the way
E verybody's happy cos you came home that day!

Jessica Harbottle (12)
Lord Lawson of Beamish School, Chester le Street

My Home Is . . .

My home is a warm environment.
My home is a safe environment.
My home is a dream come true.
My favourite room is my bedroom.
My home is like my dad, standing tall like a guard.
My home is a tidy haven in the sky.
My room makes me feel free and de-stressed.
My kitchen is a chef's palace with smells from around the world.
My living room is fab.
I feel as if I'm basking in my family's love and warmth.
My home is my den for when I come home.
My home is my chilling corner.
My home is everything I need in one place.

Katie Hill (11)
Lord Lawson of Beamish School, Chester le Street

War

I am crying . . . crying with pain
The sun's shining like a bright, white torch
But not down here in the trenches
It's raining here, pouring down actually
Here, here in no-man's-land
Bullets are flying high in the sky like little birds
The rain's gone, greyness takes over the sky
All the lights are gone now
Like being closed in a little box.

I was crying, crying with anger
Frustration taking over me
Like a blanket of anger was cuddling me
I despise the things
The things they make us do
Hungry, tired, angry and upset . . .
Upset because of the things they make us do.

I was crying, crying with happiness
All you need is your family
They're like a sunny sky hanging over you
The frustration and pain are gone now
Now that I'm home.

Nicole Hood [13]
Lord Lawson of Beamish School, Chester le Street

What Is A Home?

What is a home?
There's plenty to it.
Upstairs, downstairs,
The rooms where you sit,
Where you may lie down,
Or walk around,
Or creeping all over,
Without a sound.
A home is a home.

A home is not just a home to you,
A home is a home to your family too.
Your mother, father, brother or sister
And probably more, but I wouldn't like to list 'em.

What is a home?
It can be plenty,
A house, a flat, a tent,
Something friendly,
But no matter what it is,
It will always be a loving place.
A home is a home!

Kate Jackson (11)
Lord Lawson of Beamish School, Chester le Street

War Poem

War! War! War! How do you describe it?
Shouting, screaming and scrambling, attempting to stay alive.
A gun whistled like the paper boy as it passed,
As I stood there in a trance,
Heart pounding like a drum.
A strange sensation; my legs are numb,
Look down, all I see is mud,
Feet throbbing as I wander forward,
I step up to the front line,
Should I do this or should I not?
Load my gun. Quick! Sharp! Fast!
This could be the last.
In the trench I watch and stare,
I couldn't watch, I couldn't bear.
Pick up my stuff and head out the trench,
Guns are firing all the time.
It starts off as a jog, ends up a sprint,
A quick roll to cover!
Could be over,
Hope it's not
All of a sudden, smoke comes in,
Can't breathe, can't see,
Someone bellows, 'Grenade!'
Am I going to live? Am I going to die?
This could be goodbye.

Scott Johnson (13)
Lord Lawson of Beamish School, Chester le Street

My Home

My home is where I live
It is full of happiness, joy and love
There are toys all over the floor
Do you want to hear some more?
6 o'clock the alarm rings, ring, ring
And the day is ready to begin
There is breakfast to be got
And showers to be had
Then it's off to school for the girls
And off to work for Dad
Housework done, tea prepared, shopping complete
Mam has time to put up her feet
At 3.15 the buzzers go
And at home it's all systems go
'Homework time!' Oh no, quick, run
Dancing lessons are much more fun
Activities complete
Showers done, teeth brushed, PJs on
And it's nearly time for sleep
Goodnight kisses all around
As I walk upstairs in my dressing gown
It's lights out and all is still
Ready once again for the alarm clock's ring.

Beth Keenan (11)
Lord Lawson of Beamish School, Chester le Street

War - Why Am I Here?

Why am I here?
This isn't right.
Why am I here?
I don't want to fight.

Bloodshed, bloodshed
My body, mind and head
This isn't right, I shouldn't be here
My soul, it's dead.

My family, my friends,
I can't deal with this.
This is not who I am.
Save me, save me,
This is not who I want to be.

Bombs, the killer gas,
I cannot escape fast enough.
It's brutal.
I'm scared, but all for one and one for all,
That's what they say.

I'm like a bug crushed under a boot.
The gas has a hold of me,
Killing my insides, slowly drifting away.
The gas has a ghastly grasp of me.

Coughing, spluttering, I know what's going on.
My last thoughts:
Why does everyone come here?
I was wrong all along.

Alannah Lamb (13)
Lord Lawson of Beamish School, Chester le Street

War

It was early morning when the beam of light woke us,
Then I remembered about the war, death and destruction,
Then the mayhem of all the mines, bombs . . . and the mustard gas,
But most of all, the gunfire.
How I dreaded going out,
We all did, but we all know it's kill or be killed out here
In this treacherous land we call no-man's-land.
We call it no-man's-land because anyone and everyone that passes the barbed wire
Would be shot dead or burned alive by the flame throwers.
People call the sergeant a death god
Because all he does is kill, kill, kill.
He is unstoppable.
We would chant, 'Go Joe, go Joe!'
That was until he was shot by a sniper.
That bullet would have had me if I didn't stop.
It whistled past me and stopped the sergeant.
All I remember from that day is seeing my best friend
Shot down by a sniper, then telling his family the news.
How I hated that.

Kieran Leverett (13)
Lord Lawson of Beamish School, Chester le Street

My Hamster

My hamster is small and round.
It plays on the wheel and jumps up and down.
It likes to eat lots of food
Which probably explains why it is so chubby and fat.

My hamster likes to go in his ball.
He also likes to run into walls.
That's why I love my hamster.

Heather Arnott [13]
Ormskirk School, Ormskirk

Smoke . . .

The thick, grey coating that lines the air,
Like a big, cloudy blanket,
Trapping people like it doesn't even care . . .
Like a ginormous bomb, taking thousands of lives,
Thousands a year, but it was her that it scared . . .
It wiped out her life and my happiness too,
The day I saw her in that hospital bed,
I immediately knew that she'd soon be dead.
It saddened me deeply, but I held back the tears,
That was until she said, 'Bye-bye dears.'
When her face that loved laughter turned to dark grey
And her friendly expression was taken away,
The heart machine read out a straight line
And that was the day she was no longer mine.
Mine, my friend, I loved her dearly
And accepting she's dead, it just couldn't be!
'Bye-bye,' I whispered under my breath
And I saw her in bed when she had met death.
That saddest day in all my life,
The day when she got the knife.

Laura Taylor (13)
Ormskirk School, Ormskirk

Twisted Teachers

'Hello class!' the torturing teacher cackles,
As the children shake in their shackles.
The dinner ladies are preparing cockroaches,
As the dreaded headmaster approaches.

Shouts and screams come from 8a,
Inspectors think school is okay.
No inspector notices that this school is hell,
'Cause everyone's in English waiting for the bell.

French lessons are an extreme bore,
So are lessons three and four.
Home time is a gift from God,
I'm going home to play on CoD!

Harry Lilley (12)
Ormskirk School, Ormskirk

Spring

Spring, rain and Wellington boots,
Flowers start to sprout their roots,
Lambs are born and the sun shines down,
Puddles never leave a frown.
Love is found in February,
Sharing a tub of Ben & Jerry's.
No complaining about anything,
Because it is time to enjoy spring!

Hannah Wilson (13)
Ormskirk School, Ormskirk

Writing

It's white surface untouched,
The page is blank.
Your pen, sitting on the table,
Is wanting to stain it with its inky contents.
You pick it up,
Even though you haven't a clue what to do with it.
You press its nib against the paper
And magically it writes for you.
Its black ink loops and swirls
Around the page forming letters.
Finally, the beautiful black formations
Come to an end
And you find
You have this poem on the page.

Emma Harden (12)
Ormskirk School, Ormskirk

World's Greatest Mum

My mum is the one who cleans my room,
She sweeps up dirt with a broom.
I love my mum very much,
She's the one I depend on to cook.

I am number one, I want to be the best son.
That's another reason I love my mum,
She shines like a star,
Even though she can't drive a car.

She's soft, she's squeezy and doesn't mind,
But my brother's running riot all the time.
So I would hug her many more times,
'Cause she's the world's greatest and best mum
And she is mine.

Brandon Slater (13)
Ormskirk School, Ormskirk

My Family

My family are always there for me,
Even when I hurt my knee.
They keep me healthy, they keep me strong,
They are always there when I do wrong.
They are always there whatever I do,
They make me better when I have the flu.

My family are always funny,
Even when the day's not sunny.
They make me laugh, they make me cry,
They even make me apple pie.
When I am sad they cheer me up,
They even buy me a special cup.

My brother is a big hugger,
My sister is a big lover.
My parents are so kind,
They can even read my mind.

Kelly Rutland (13) & Bethan Johnson (13)
Ormskirk School, Ormskirk

Eczema

Itching, itching, scratching, scratching
Bright red like fire burning
An active volcano exploding
A devil's trident tail stabbing
Blood drips like lava flowing
Sharp thorns instead of roses swaying
Slap on the cream - that will be soothing
Cream calms. Now back to normal.
Phew!

Jamie Dalby (12)
Ormskirk School, Ormskirk

The Haunted House

The haunted house in which I stayed a night
To prove to my friends that it didn't give me a fright
I dragged my bag across the floor
To reach the old, mite-ridden door
I pushed and pushed with all my might
Eventually it opened just a slight.

I unpacked the things I needed the most
At the corner of my eye - did I see a ghost?
I stumbled across the hallowed hall
To the end of the stairs where I did fall
And there, sat by the door
Was the thing that scared me most of all.

It chased me and chased me round the house
I screamed, but it came out quiet as a mouse
I ran so fast all the way home
But even then I wasn't alone
There in my room, on my bed
Sat a teddy bear with no head.

Antonia Jenkins (12)
Ormskirk School, Ormskirk

Chocolate

Bubbly, bubbly, melt in the mouth
As it curls in and out of your tongue
It sings as you hum
What angels have sung
To brighten up every day.

Milk, dark, white
All for me
The taste throws a bash
Like a star in the night
It runs like a man in a marathon in the mouth.

Smooth as silk
Creamy as milk
I'm so excited for tonight
When I can begin
This is all for me
This is not just chocolate
This is my chocolate!

Emma Hill
Ormskirk School, Ormskirk

Underground

There trapped,
Caught by terror,
Herded in like sheep,
The soil their sheepdog.

A glimmer of light their survival hole,
Their hope at the end of the tunnel,
Their family's lifeline,
Their children's childhood.

The soil acts like a crumbly apple pie,
Hot and cold,
Moist and dry,
Still yet moving.

They remain brave,
But inside their hearts shatter like glass.
One by one they clamber up the tube,
Their prison sentence is finally over.
Freedom is there to welcome them.
The Chilean miners.

Alexandra Sines (12)
Ormskirk School, Ormskirk

What The Tortured Know

Torture, a word that rings hell
Into their ears,
Makes them scream,
Wakes them up in the night,
It scars them mentally
And physically.

It makes people laugh,
It makes people cry,
The tortured know
That soon they will die.

Torture is painful,
Long and drawn out,
Torture is a disease,
It kills without a doubt.

Lying in a pit,
Disease will eat at you,
Lying on the floor,
Things are thrown at you.

The number one killer in the 1500's,
Bones shattering,
Teeth chattering.

Thomas Phillips (13)
Ormskirk School, Ormskirk

Joy

Snow-covered slopes
Like a glittering snow globe
An icy hand
Has passed over the land
Covering all with snow.

The children plead, 'Can I go? Can I go?'
And so, they emerge
Like some power surge
Has made them get all ready
When they reach the slope they shout, 'Ready? Steady? . . .

Go!' Zooming, zooming down the slope
With cold all around, can they cope?
Pushed by the ice,
They scream, 'Isn't it nice?'
All day, all night, they go down and down.

When I wander into town
During this magical time
I see that on everyone's face, the line
Is curved, they are content, not stressed.
Only snow could bring such happiness.

Jonathan Coney [12]
Ormskirk School, Ormskirk

The Crowd Roared

The crowd roared like a pack of lions,
As the players entered the field.
The Everton fans were as hard as irons,
As the Liverpool fans were very wild.
The Everton fans sang happily in joy
As Cahill scored again, my golden boy.

Cahill, Cahill, what a goal,
He scored it with his newborn sole.
The Liverpool fans were as quiet as a mouse,
And I now wanted to party at my house.
Second half had come and gone,
But we only had one.

Everton scored a cracker again,
Now surely we had the game.
Two to none, nobody was
Expecting that one.
The parties started, woo, whay,
Now I could get drunk and lie in some hay.

Tom Atherton (13)
Ormskirk School, Ormskirk

The Day of The Big Game

It was the day of the big game,
Two teams both playing for their fame,
Fans were ready,
Players were ready,
It was the day of the big game.

It was the day of the big game,
Mascots playing the role of the dame,
Drunken fans could not stand
Listening to the beat of the band,
It was the day of the big game.

It was the day of the big game,
The roar of the crowd,
Shook all around,
In Mexican waves around the ground.

It was the end of the big game,
The whistle was blown in shame,
The crowd stopped roaring,
It was like you could hear a pin drop.
We had lost the big game.

Rachel Dickinson (13)
Ormskirk School, Ormskirk

Drugs

Drugs, just one word,
Yet powerful enough to
Change everything
You've ever known.

I knew someone, once,
She was sweet and kind and caring,
Talented, thoughtful and always laughing,
She was my auntie, my friend.

Then, within a week,
All contact was cut off.
They thought they were protecting me,
But I didn't understand.

My world was happy, bright,
And I was full of hope.
But then I heard that one, devastating word,
And my world was dead and gone.

I was introduced to pain,
Cruelty and hate.
This happy little girl
Not so happy anymore.

I hated what it did to her,
And for a while I hated her.
My cousins lived in fear and hatred,
Wondering if she'd be home at night.

Then the social workers stepped in,
We had to do something.
It was getting out of control
And we all feared their verdict.

For a while the twins, 2 out of the 7,
Lived with us.
But they had changed.
Where joy and playfulness once lived,
Grief and fear and sadness lurked.

About a year ago she died
And so did I a bit.
It changed all of our lives
And now we cry at night.

Drugs, one word,
Yet powerful enough
To change everything
I've ever known.

Connie Murray-Moon (13)
Ormskirk School, Ormskirk

Waiting

I see the crowd approaching,
The hustle and bustle at its peak,
Chatty teenagers, businessmen,
All talking to people in their own speak.

Babies cry like foghorns,
Adding to the atmosphere,
Trainspotters looking for the 752,
Mums waving children goodbye,
(Their loud cries for the umpteenth time.)

Guards shouting,
'Wait, you haven't paid!'
An elderly couple make their way
Carefully to the front.

As I draw up to the stop,
All I can see
Are all the faces,
Of those waiting, waiting for me . . .

I am the one,
The one with the power
And without me,
They'd be late by the hour.

I am the train,
As fast as an eagle,
Speedy like a cheetah,
Arriving on time once again!

Anna Donnelly (12)
Ormskirk School, Ormskirk

The Gymnastics Competition

Silently the music played,
The gymnast swayed.
Shimmering, Swarovski leotard,
Like stars in the night sky,
As the audience wept a silent cry.
The music had stopped,
The gymnast had finished,
A seal of approval was given.
Clap, clap, clap, clap,
The audience snapped to the next performance.
Silently, the music played,
The gymnast swayed.

Ella Burgess (12)
Ormskirk School, Ormskirk

Untitled

If I could but give it
To the child on the street
For food, for shelter
And shoes for his feet.

If I could but give it
To the woman who cries
Who withstands the beatings
Then hides them with lies.

If I could but give it,
To the man who can't see,
Who relies on his dog
For guidance, for love, for the freedom to be.

If I could but give it,
To the girl who won't walk,
Who's waiting for treatment,
While the doctors, frustrated, constantly talk.

If I did but give it,
To those most in need,
Who would help the rest?
Would we succeed?

Kelly Schweizer (15)
Polam Hall School, Darlington

Imagination

Imagination is the best present,
Imagination is the worst gift,
Imagination lets you soar above the clouds,
On the smoothest ocean, you are able to drift.

Imagination is the best thought,
Imagination is the worst idea,
Imagination lets you swim in the deepest sea,
Travel to lands far and near.

Imagination is the best dance,
Imagination is the worst twirl,
Imagination lets you touch the most secretive souls,
It can help you, give it a swirl!

Imagination is the best present,
Imagination is the worst gift.

Heidi Leigh (12)
Polam Hall School, Darlington

Lovely Mommy

Loves and smiles,
Talks a while,
Lovely, lovely Mommy.
Helps and shares,
Great ideas,
Lovely, lovely Mommy.
When I'm down,
She's around,
Lovely, lovely Mommy.
There is one thing I love most,
That she's mine!

Courtney Hillman (12)
St Leonard's Catholic School, Durham

Freedom

I am the one who held those men
Deep inside of me they lay
Side by side, their burden heavy
The burden I had to carry.
I mourned out loud as I felt their pain
They had rights, but protested in vain.
I split up many families by what I did,
But I had no choice; I was in their hands,
Different men, faces as white as the moon
That I passed under many a night.
When I came over the horizon, depression I brought
Along with hard workers, from which many were bought.
What became of them I cannot say,
Only the pure distaste of what I did.
I would even suffer instead of them,
Sunken on the seabed
Among the dead.
Many curses against me,
But I don't blame them.
I wanted to give them their freedom,
Even that I could not do.
I cannot say what I most regret,
I am a slave ship, many an unfree man I met.

Esther Bancroft (12)
St Leonard's Catholic School, Durham

Rotto

A world of a thousand broken emotions,
A crooked smile dismayingly false,
A melancholy giggle, too destitute for words' tight grip.
Falsity, conquering the air in our lustrous lungs,
Our safety harness worn too tight, paralysed from any movement,
So desperately, essentially needed before extinction of love.
Love?
Your love was as strong as the bonds of a chain.
Each piece so effortlessly forged until finally, your masterpiece of compassion.
Misfortune, striking your frail hearts, the rotting of your heart's survival,
Slowly disintegrating all signs of happiness.
Gasping, choking, drowning in a sea of optimistic misery,
A fight for survival, but the ticking of a tormenting clock.

Sophie Dellapina (17)
St Leonard's Catholic School, Durham

What Matters To Me

What matters to me,
Family and friends,
Will be together till the very end,
What matters to me, what matters to me,
Read this poem and you will see.

What matters to me,
Food and water,
What matters to me,
My sister's daughter,
What matters to me, what matters to me,
Read this poem and you will see.

What matters to me,
That there is no crime, this brings world peace,
And we're all fine,
What matters to me, what matters to me,
Read this poem and you will see.

What matters to me,
Christmas presents,
Sitting round the table eating turkey and pheasants,
What matters to me, what matters to me,
Read this poem and you will see.

Rebecca Quigley (12)
Sale High School, Sale

Love Me

L isten to me
O nly I can explain how I feel
V enting is what I find hard to do
E xploring my possibilities

M ay give some hope
E xplaining might help you love me.

Ryan North (14)
The Grange Learning Centre, Low Willington

Dying

I thought the Deads were tough,
I thought the Deads were cool,
But then I ended up in a blood pool,
So now I know they are nothing to me,
Next time you wanna be a gangsta,
Think of me strapped to a respirator.
Brother I'm telling you stick in at school,
Don't end up in a blood pool,
Get yourself a life,
Get yourself a wife,
Get yourself a job and a cool new hob,
But whatever, don't end up a piece of meat,
Lying, dying on the cold, uncaring street.
They had no reason to do me in,
I felt as if I'd been chucked in the bin.

Daniel Peters (15)
Windlestone Hall School, Ferryhill

A Love Of My Own

What matters to me is a love of my own,
But half the time it is scared to be shown,
The blood and the tears that make these songs
As well as the sound of the gongs.

The first song, 'The Servant Of Evil',
It makes you think, is this believable?
The second song is a favourite of mine,
It is sung by a boy called Len Kagamine.
He sings of a sinful child,
Whose mind went completely wild.
He murdered those close to him
And ended up dead instead of his sibling, Rin.

The third song is loud and heavy,
It talks of a war getting ready.
The girl in blue, she screams out loud
For the love of her life is never found.

The song that makes me cry the most is about a girl and her sad woes.
She sings of her brother and of her foes.
She sings of sadness, of fear, but never joy,
Because she fell in love with this boy.

Enough I say of these sad, sinful songs,
Instead I'll talk of another one;
The song talks of being together with someone
Who makes you feel like you belong,
But vocaloid is not the only love I have.
I also have lucky star and its funny cast:
With the hyperactive Konata,
The cute and cuddly Tukasa,
And the fury of Kagameme and the brains of miyuki,
'Oh, lucky star, I adore ya!'
And then I have another love,
By the mane of Haruhi and the quiet Yuki.
They form the SOS Brigade,
And search for things that are not in the shade.

The last love I have cherished for years.
Now when I think about it, it brings me to tears.

But not tears of sadness but tears of joy
You could say it's my favourite kind of toy.
My last love is DDR,
I never think of it as Sub-Par,
The arrows flash and rise to the top,
When I start playing, I never want to stop.

These loves are of my own
But now they don't mind being shown,
You see in my life I have many likes
But Manga and Anime are my only loves.

Jordan Ward (15)
Windlestone Hall School, Ferryhill

Fishing

Fishing is my thing,
I like it a lot.
The only thing I dislike,
Is the one I never got!

I like to go fishing all about
To try and catch big brown trout.

The salmon put up a big fight,
I need to use all my might.
They do not like big bright light.
You're better off going out at night.

Big fish, little fish, I like them a lot,
I don't care; I want them in my pot.
The reel is screaming,
The rod is bent double . . . is it going to pull me in?
I'm in big trouble.

Steven Jaye (15)
Windlestone Hall School, Ferryhill